THE HISTORY OF MONEY

MONEY

Patricia Armentrout

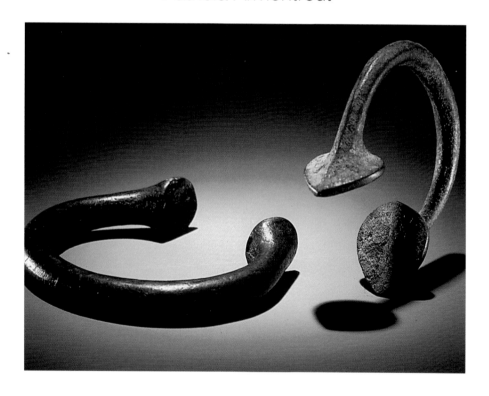

The Rourke Press, Inc.
Vero Beach, Florida 32964

PHOTO CREDITS
© Armentrout: pgs. 4, 18; © The Smithsonian Institution National
Numismatic Collection: Cover, Title, pgs. 8, 10, 12, 13, 15, 17; ©
Elwin Trump: pg. 21; © Oscar C. Williams: pg. 7

ACKNOWLEDGMENTS
The author acknowledges David Armentrout for his contribution in
writing this book.

Library of Congress Cataloging-in-Publication Data

Armentrout, Patricia, 1960 -
   The history of money / by Patricia Armentrout
     p. cm. — (Money)
   Includes index.
   Summary: Examines the history of money, including the barter
system, early trade in North America, unusual types of money such
as huge stone disks and salt bars, and the first paper money.
   ISBN 1-57103-118-9
   1. Money—History—Juvenile literature. [1. Money—History.]
I. Title II. Series: Armentrout, Patricia, 1960 -   Money.
HG221.5.A69 1996
332.4' 9—dc20   96–4575
                                                CIP
                                                AC

Printed in the USA

TABLE OF CONTENTS

LIFE WITHOUT MONEY

Long ago, people did not use money. They didn't need it. People built their own houses, hunted, and grew their own crops.

Then people began to work at what they did best. People who were good at working with wood made furniture for others. Crop farmers grew more so they could provide food to non-farmers. People worked at what they did best and traded goods or services with each other. This trade is called **barter** (BAR ter).

Kids use the barter system when trading baseball cards

THE BARTER SYSTEM

Bartering was the first system of payment, and it was used all over the world. Bartering goods and services worked well only when people agreed on the **value** (VAL yoo) of what was traded.

Two farmers might agree to trade a sack of wheat for a bushel of corn, if they agreed that wheat and corn had the same value.

In many countries food can be sold or traded for other items of value

EARLY TRADE IN NORTH AMERICA

Native Americans traded beaded belts made from purple and white clam shells. The belts, called **wampum** (WAHM pem), were used to settle agreements between villages.

Beaver pelts and other animal skins were often used in trade. Animal skins were used to make clothing for protection against the cold weather.

Cocoa beans, the kind used to make chocolate, were often used as money in Mexican villages.

Many years ago these beaver skins and shell beads were used as money

UNUSUAL MONEY

Can you imagine paying for something with a huge stone disk over 10 feet wide? **Ancient** (AIN shent) people from Yap, a South Pacific island, did just that.

Ancient Chinese people often traded **cowrie** (COW ree) shells for food and clothing. The people of Ethiopia, an Eastern African country, used salt bars in trade.

Some countries traded items made from metals. Egypt used gold ring money when bartering.

Stone disks weighing as much as 500 pounds were used as money on the Island of Yap

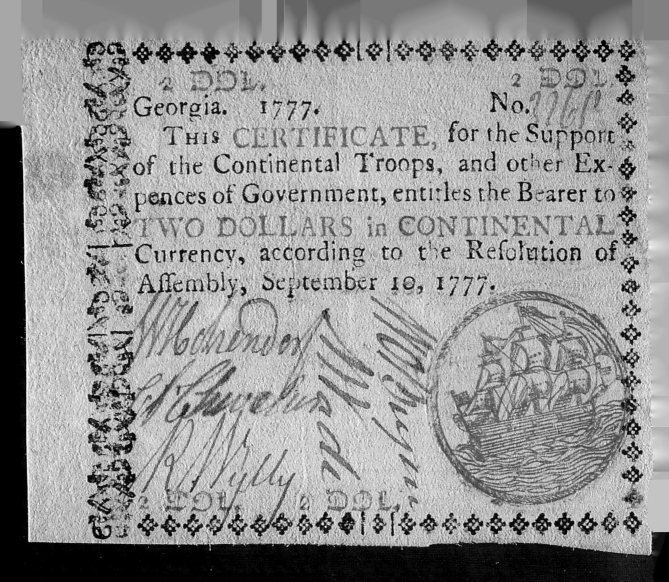

2 DOL.

Georgia. 1777.

No.

THIS CERTIFICATE, for the Support of the Continental Troops, and other Expences of Government, entitles the Bearer to TWO DOLLARS in CONTINENTAL Currency, according to the Resolution of Assembly, September 10, 1777.

An American Georgia $2 certificate issued in 1777

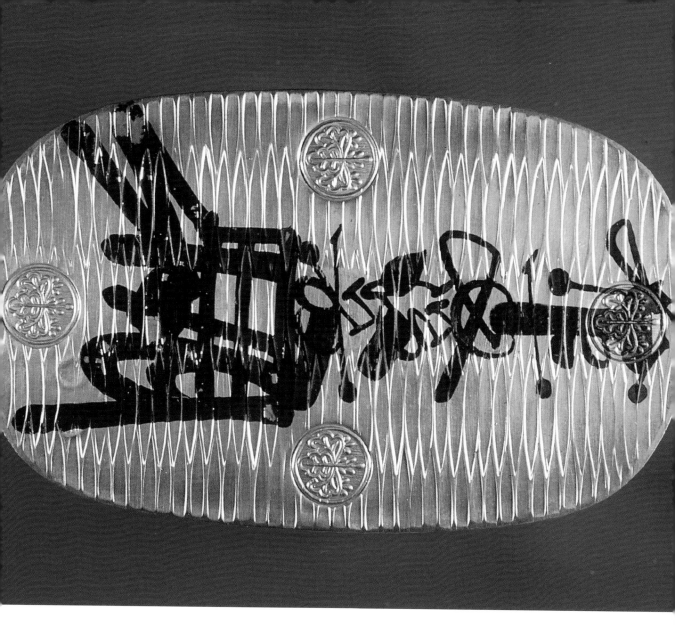

Japanese oban were used in trade just like money is today

THE FIRST COINS

Metal objects were popular in trade because metal is very strong.

Standard sized coins were made by melting metal and pouring the hot metal into molds. Coins made with the same metals and the same size molds would weigh the same. Those coins had the same value, or worth.

All coins were not round. Some early Japanese and Roman coins were rectangular. Some early Chinese coins were shaped like tools and seashells.

People in Egypt valued gold and made ring money from it

THE BEGINNING OF PAPER MONEY

Paper money was invented because people grew tired of carrying large, heavy coins. Ancient Chinese store owners gave handwritten receipts to people who wanted their coins stored in one place.

The Chinese government liked the idea of paper receipts. The government began to print paper notes with values that equaled several coins.

Soon trade ships carried paper notes instead of coins, and the use of paper money spread to the Western world.

The Chinese people were among the first to use paper money

ANCIENT BANKS

A long time ago, people stored their money in **temples** (TEM pulz). They believed no one would steal from a sacred place.

Temple workers loaned money to people in need. The temple workers began to loan more money to more people when they realized they could charge a fee for the loan.

Today, as in ancient times, money is borrowed from banks for a fee called **interest** (IN trest).

Banks are now the common place to deposit money for saving

THE GOLD STANDARD

Although silver, bronze, and copper were valuable metals, gold became popular because it is rare, or hard to find.

Gold was so popular in many countries that governments based the value of money on gold. Governments would back up, or guarantee, their paper money's value with gold. This "gold standard" made trade easy among countries.

These U. S. gold coins were made in the 19th Century

EARNING MONEY

Without money, people would not be able to provide their families with food, shelter, and clothing.

Today people earn money by working for it. Grocery store managers hire people to stock shelves, schools hire teachers, and teenagers earn money by baby-sitting and shoveling snow.

Because money is earned and spent in nearly every country in the world, it has been said that "money makes the world go around."

Glossary

ancient (AIN shent) — very old; from times long ago

barter (BAR ter) — to trade by exchanging goods or services

cowrie (COW ree) — a sea shell

interest (IN trest) — a charge for borrowing money

temples (TEM pulz) — places people go to worship

value (VAL yoo) — the amount of money something is worth or the fair exchange for something

wampum (WAHM pem) — shell beads on strings used as money by Native Americans

INDEX

DATE DUE

OC 28			